delicious diabetic
recipes

Savory Sandwiches

Table of Contents

Open-Faced Reubens

  1 **cup shredded cabbage**
  2 **tablespoons light mayonnaise, divided**
  2 **tablespoons reduced-sodium or no-salt-added chili sauce, divided**
  4 **slices pumpernickel or rye bread, toasted**
  4 **ounces sliced pastrami**
  2 **slices reduced-fat Swiss cheese, cut into ½-inch strips**

1. Preheat broiler. Combine cabbage, 1 tablespoon mayonnaise and 1 tablespoon chili sauce in medium bowl; mix well.

2. Stir remaining 1 tablespoon mayonnaise and 1 tablespoon chili sauce in small bowl until well blended. Spread mayonnaise mixture over bread slices. Top each with 1 ounce pastrami, ¼ cup cabbage mixture and one fourth of cheese strips. Place on baking sheet.

3. Broil 4 to 5 inches from heat source 40 seconds to 1 minute or until cheese is melted. Serve immediately.   *Makes 4 servings*

Serving Size: 1 reuben
Calories 164, **Total Fat** 4g, **Saturated Fat** 2g,
Protein 12g, **Carbohydrate** 21g, **Cholesterol** 24mg,
Dietary Fiber 3g, **Sodium** 670mg

Dietary Exchanges: 1 Starch, 1 Vegetable, 1 Meat

Grilled Portobello and Spring Green Sandwiches

        2 tablespoons extra virgin olive oil
    1½ tablespoons balsamic vinegar
        1 tablespoon Dijon mustard
        1 tablespoon water
        1 teaspoon dried oregano
        1 clove garlic, minced
        ½ teaspoon black pepper
        ¼ teaspoon salt
        4 large portobello mushroom caps, stems removed
        8 slices (1 ounce each) multigrain Italian bread
        ¼ cup crumbled reduced-fat blue cheese
        2 to 3 ounces spring greens

1. Whisk oil, vinegar, mustard, water, oregano, garlic, pepper and salt in medium bowl until well blended. Place mushrooms on sheet of foil or large plate. Brush 2 tablespoons dressing over mushrooms; set remaining dressing aside. Marinate 30 minutes.

2. Spray grill pan with nonstick cooking spray; heat over medium-high heat. Spray both sides of bread slices with cooking spray. Grill bread 1 minute per side, pressing down with spatula until bread is toasted. Set aside.

3. Grill mushrooms 3 to 4 minutes per side or until tender. Place each mushroom on 1 bread slice. Sprinkle with blue cheese.

4. Combine spring greens and reserved dressing; toss to coat evenly. Arrange spring greens on top of mushrooms; top with remaining bread slices. Serve immediately.   *Makes 4 sandwiches*

Serving Size: 1 sandwich
Calories 275, **Total Fat** 10g, **Saturated Fat** 2g,
Protein 9g, **Carbohydrate** 36g, **Cholesterol** 4mg,
Dietary Fiber 3g, **Sodium** 590mg

Dietary Exchanges: 2 Starch, 2 Fat, 1 Vegetable

Mediterranean Sandwiches

1¼ pounds chicken tenders, cut crosswise in half

1 large tomato, cut into bite-size pieces

½ small cucumber, halved lengthwise, seeded and sliced

½ cup sliced onion

2 tablespoons cider vinegar

1 tablespoon olive or canola oil

3 teaspoons minced fresh oregano *or* ½ teaspoon dried oregano

2 teaspoons minced fresh mint *or* ¼ teaspoon dried mint

¼ teaspoon salt

6 (6-inch) whole wheat pita bread rounds, cut in half crosswise

1. Spray large nonstick skillet with nonstick cooking spray; heat over medium heat. Add chicken; cook and stir 7 to 10 minutes or no longer pink. Let stand 5 to 10 minutes to cool slightly.

2. Combine chicken, tomato, cucumber and onion in medium bowl. Add vinegar, oil, oregano, mint and salt; gently toss to coat.

3. Divide chicken mixture evenly among pita bread halves.

Makes 6 servings

Serving Size: 2 filled pita bread halves
Calories 242, **Total Fat** 6g, **Saturated Fat** 1g,
Protein 23g, **Carbohydrate** 24g, **Cholesterol** 50mg,
Dietary Fiber 2g, **Sodium** 353mg

Dietary Exchanges: 1½ Starch, 2½ Meat

Ham & Egg Breakfast Panini

¼ cup chopped red or green bell pepper

2 tablespoons sliced green onion

1 slice (1 ounce) reduced-fat smoked deli ham, chopped

½ cup cholesterol-free egg substitute

Dash black pepper

4 slices multigrain or whole grain bread

2 slices (¾ ounce each) reduced-fat Cheddar or Swiss cheese

1. Spray small skillet with nonstick cooking spray; heat over medium heat. Add bell pepper and green onion; cook and stir 4 minutes or until crisp-tender. Stir in ham.

2. Whisk egg substitute and black pepper in small bowl until well blended. Pour egg mixture into skillet; cook 2 minutes or until egg mixture is almost set, stirring occasionally.

3. Heat grill pan or medium skillet over medium heat. Top 2 bread slices with 1 cheese slice and half of egg mixture. Top with remaining 2 bread slices. Spray sandwiches with cooking spray.

4. Grill sandwiches 2 minutes per side, pressing down lightly with spatula until cheese is melted and bread is toasted. (Cover pan with lid during last 2 minutes of cooking to melt cheese, if desired.) Serve immediately.

Makes 2 sandwiches

Serving Size: 1 sandwich
Calories 271, **Total Fat** 5g, **Saturated Fat** 1g,
Protein 24g, **Carbohydrate** 30g, **Cholesterol** 9mg,
Dietary Fiber 6g, **Sodium** 577mg

Dietary Exchanges: 2 Starch, 2 Meat

Turkey & Vegetable Roll-Ups

¾ pound turkey breast cutlets or tenderloin, cut into strips

2 cloves garlic, minced

½ teaspoon chili powder

2 teaspoons canola oil

½ cup thinly sliced yellow onion

1 yellow or red bell pepper, cut into strips

1 small zucchini, thinly sliced (about 1 cup)

½ cup chunky salsa

4 medium (7- to 8-inch) whole wheat tortillas, warmed

½ cup (2 ounces) shredded reduced-fat Mexican cheese blend

¼ cup chopped fresh cilantro (optional)

1. Combine turkey, garlic and chili powder in medium bowl; toss to coat.

2. Heat oil in large nonstick skillet over medium-high heat. Add onion and bell pepper; cook and stir 2 minutes. Add zucchini; cook and stir 1 minute. Add turkey; cook and stir 4 minutes or until turkey is no longer pink and vegetables are tender. Reduce heat to medium-low; stir in salsa. Cook 2 minutes.

3. Spoon turkey mixture onto tortillas; top with cheese and cilantro, if desired. Roll up to enclose filling. Serve immediately. *Makes 4 servings*

Serving Size: 1 roll-up
Calories 333, **Total Fat** 9g, **Saturated Fat** 2g,
Protein 30g, **Carbohydrate** 30g, **Cholesterol** 43mg,
Dietary Fiber 4g, **Sodium** 450mg

Dietary Exchanges: 2 Starch, 1 Vegetable, 3 Meat

Chicken Salad Pitas with Yogurt Sauce

- 1½ cups finely chopped cooked chicken breast
- ½ cup halved red seedless grapes
- 1 stalk celery, chopped
- 2½ tablespoons plain nonfat Greek yogurt
- 2 tablespoons fat-free mayonnaise
- ¼ teaspoon salt
- ⅛ teaspoon curry powder
- ⅛ teaspoon chili powder
- ⅛ teaspoon black pepper
- 2 (6-inch) whole wheat pita bread rounds, cut in half crosswise
- 4 lettuce leaves
- 1 tablespoon sliced almonds

1. Combine chicken, grapes and celery in medium bowl. Stir yogurt, mayonnaise, salt, curry powder, chili powder and pepper in small bowl until well blended. Spoon over chicken mixture; toss to coat evenly.

2. Line each pita bread half with lettuce. Spoon ½ cup chicken mixture into each pita half; sprinkle with 1½ teaspoons sliced almonds.   *Makes 4 servings*

Serving Size: 1 filled pita bread half
Calories 178, **Total Fat** 3g, **Saturated Fat** 1g,
Protein 20g, **Carbohydrate** 20g, **Cholesterol** 41mg,
Dietary Fiber 3g, **Sodium** 410mg

Dietary Exchanges: 1 Starch, 1 Meat

Mediterranean Tuna Sandwiches

1 can (12 ounces) solid white tuna packed in water, drained and flaked

¼ cup finely chopped red onion

¼ cup fat-free or low-fat mayonnaise

3 tablespoons chopped black olives

1 tablespoon plus 1 teaspoon lemon juice

1 tablespoon chopped fresh mint (optional)

1 tablespoon olive oil

¼ teaspoon black pepper

⅛ teaspoon garlic powder (optional)

8 slices whole wheat bread

4 pieces romaine lettuce

4 thin slices tomato

1. Combine tuna, onion, mayonnaise, olives, lemon juice, mint, if desired, oil, pepper and garlic powder, if desired, in large bowl until combined.

2. Top 4 bread slices with lettuce and tomato. Spoon ⅔ cup tuna mixture over each tomato. Top with remaining 4 bread slices.   *Makes 4 sandwiches*

Serving Size: 1 sandwich
Calories 332, **Total Fat** 12g, **Saturated Fat** 2g,
Protein 29g, **Carbohydrate** 27g, **Cholesterol** 31mg,
Dietary Fiber 4g, **Sodium** 483mg

Dietary Exchanges: 1½ Starch, ½ Vegetable, 3½ Meat

Mushroom, Ham and Cheese Sandwiches

- **2** cups sliced mushrooms
- Dash salt (optional)
- Dash black pepper
- Dash dried rosemary
- **2** tablespoons low-fat mayonnaise
- **4** slices whole wheat bread, toasted
- **2** slices 96% fat-free, reduced-sodium ham
- **2** thin slices reduced-fat Swiss cheese

1. Spray large skillet with nonstick cooking spray; heat over medium-high heat. Add mushrooms; cook and stir 5 minutes or until lightly browned. Sprinkle with salt, if desired, pepper and rosemary.

2. Spread mayonnaise on half of bread slices. Top evenly with mushrooms, ham, cheese and remaining bread slices. Serve immediately.

Makes 2 sandwiches

Serving Size: 1 sandwich
Calories 263, **Total Fat** 8g, **Saturated Fat** 3g,
Protein 19g, **Carbohydrate** 32g, **Cholesterol** 20mg,
Dietary Fiber 3g, **Sodium** 619mg,

Dietary Exchanges: 2 Starch, ½ Fat, 2 Meat

Garbanzo Sandwich Bundles

¼ cup ketchup

1 tablespoon red wine vinegar

1 teaspoon dried fines herbes*

1 teaspoon Dijon mustard

⅛ teaspoon black pepper

1 can (about 15 ounces) reduced-sodium chickpeas, rinsed and drained

1 cup sliced mushrooms

8 cherry tomatoes, quartered

½ cup shredded carrots

½ cup (2 ounces) shredded reduced-fat Swiss cheese

4 large (10-inch) flour tortillas

8 lettuce leaves

Fines herbes is a combination of herbs commonly used in Mediterranean cooking. You may substitute with ¼ teaspoon each: dried parsley, dried chervil, dried tarragon and freeze-dried chives.

1. Combine ketchup, vinegar, fines herbes, mustard and pepper in medium bowl. Stir in chickpeas, mushrooms, tomatoes, carrots and cheese.

2. Line each tortilla with 2 lettuce leaves. Spoon evenly with chickpea mixture. Roll up to enclose filling.   *Makes 4 servings*

Serving Size: 1 sandwich bundle
Calories 277, **Total Fat** 7g, **Saturated Fat** 1g,
Protein 14g, **Carbohydrate** 43g, **Cholesterol** 7mg,
Dietary Fiber 8g, **Sodium** 660mg

Dietary Exchanges: 2½ Starch, 1 Fat, 1 Vegetable, ½ Meat

Heavenly Cranberry Turkey Sandwiches

- ¼ cup light cream cheese
- ¼ cup cranberry sauce or chutney
- 2 tablespoons chopped walnuts, toasted*
- 8 slices multigrain or whole wheat bread, lightly toasted
- ½ pound sliced deli smoked turkey breast
- 1 cup packed mesclun or spring salad mixed greens *or* 4 red leaf lettuce leaves

To toast walnuts, spread in single layer on baking sheet. Bake in preheated 350°F oven 5 to 7 minutes or until fragrant, stirring occasionally.

1. Combine cream cheese and cranberry sauce in small bowl; mix well. Stir in walnuts.

2. Spread mixture on bread slices. Layer turkey and greens on 4 bread slices; top with remaining 4 bread slices. Serve immediately.   *Makes 4 sandwiches*

Serving Size: 1 sandwich
Calories 291, **Total Fat** 8g, **Saturated Fat** 2g,
Protein 20g, **Carbohydrate** 39g, **Cholesterol** 28mg,
Dietary Fiber 9g, **Sodium** 698mg

Dietary Exchanges: 2 Starch, ½ Fruit, 2 Meat

Summer Tomato and Cheese Melts

2 tablespoons low-fat mayonnaise

2 teaspoons prepared pesto

4 slices (1 ounce each) whole grain bread

4 tomato slices (about ¼ inch thick)

4 thin cucumber slices (about 3 inches long)

2 slices part-skim mozzarella cheese

1. Combine mayonnaise and pesto in small bowl; spread evenly on 2 bread slices. Top with tomato, cucumber, cheese and remaining bread slices.

2. Spray grill pan or large skillet with nonstick cooking spray; heat over medium heat. Cook sandwiches about 3 to 4 minutes per side, pressing down with spatula until cheese is melted and bread is toasted. (Cover pan during last minute of cooking to melt cheese, if desired.) Serve immediately.

Makes 2 sandwiches

Serving Size: 1 sandwich
Calories 226, **Total Fat** 7g, **Saturated Fat** 2g,
Protein 12g, **Carbohydrate** 33g, **Cholesterol** 13mg,
Dietary Fiber 5g, **Sodium** 506mg

Dietary Exchanges: 2 Starch, ½ Fat, 1 Meat

Pesto Tuna Melts

  1 can (5 ounces) tuna in water, drained and flaked
  1 tablespoon plain nonfat Greek yogurt
  1 tablespoon pesto sauce
  1 teaspoon lemon juice
  ⅛ teaspoon black pepper
  2 light multi-grain English muffins, split
  4 tomato slices
  6 teaspoons shredded reduced-fat mozzarella cheese

1. Preheat oven to 350°F.

2. Combine tuna, yogurt, pesto, lemon juice and pepper in small bowl; gently mix.

3. Divide tuna mixture evenly among English muffin halves. Top each half with 1 tomato slice and 1½ teaspoons cheese.

4. Bake 8 to 10 minutes or until cheese is melted. Serve immediately.

Makes 2 servings

Serving Size: 2 topped English muffin halves
Calories 252, **Total Fat** 6g, **Saturated Fat** 1g,
Protein 27g, **Carbohydrate** 27g, **Cholesterol** 27mg,
Dietary Fiber 8g, **Sodium** 612mg

Dietary Exchanges: 2 Starch, 3 Meat

Roasted Eggplant Panini

- 1 medium eggplant (about 1¼ pounds)
- 1 cup (4 ounces) shredded reduced-fat mozzarella cheese
- 1 tablespoon chopped fresh basil
- 1 tablespoon fresh lemon juice
- ⅛ teaspoon salt
- 8 slices (1 ounce each) whole grain Italian bread

1. Preheat oven to 400°F. Line baking sheet with parchment paper; spray with nonstick cooking spray. Slice eggplant in half lengthwise. Place cut sides down on prepared baking sheet. Roast 45 minutes. Let stand 15 minutes or until cool enough to handle.

2. Meanwhile, combine cheese, basil, lemon juice and salt in small bowl; set aside.

3. Cut each eggplant piece in half. Remove pulp; discard skin. Place one fourth of eggplant on each of 4 bread slices, pressing gently into bread. Top evenly with cheese mixture. Top with remaining bread slices. Spray sandwiches with nonstick cooking spray.

4. Heat large nonstick skillet or grill pan over medium heat. Cook sandwiches 3 to 4 minutes per side, pressing down with spatula until cheese is melted and bread is toasted. (Cover pan during last minute of cooking to melt cheese, if desired.) Serve immediately.   *Makes 4 sandwiches*

Serving Size: 1 sandwich
Calories 310, **Total Fat** 7g, **Saturated Fat** 2g,
Protein 19g, **Carbohydrate** 50g, **Cholesterol** 10mg,
Dietary Fiber 9g, **Sodium** 275mg

Dietary Exchanges: 3 Starch, 2 Meat

Smoked Salmon Spirals

    2 tablespoons low-fat cream cheese
    1 light sun-dried tomato flatbread
    2 ounces smoked salmon (lox)
    ½ cup baby arugula
    ½ cup thinly sliced red bell pepper

Spread cream cheese on flatbread. Layer with smoked salmon, arugula and bell pepper. Roll up jelly-roll style. To serve, cut into 6 pieces.

Makes 2 servings

Serving Size: 3 spirals
Calories 121, **Total Fat** 5g, **Saturated Fat** 2g,
Protein 11g, **Carbohydrate** 12g, **Cholesterol** 15mg,
Dietary Fiber 5g, **Sodium** 800mg

Dietary Exchanges: 1 Starch, 1 Meat